UNDERWATER ORIGAMI

STEVE AND MEGUMI BIDDLE

Illustrations by Megumi Biddle

BARRON'S

First edition for the United States and Canada published by Barron's Educational Series, Inc., 2000.
First published in Great Britain in 1999 by Red Fox Books, Random House Children's Books, 20 Vauxhall Bridge Road, London SW1V 2SA
Text © Steve and Megumi Biddle 1999, Illustrations © Megumi Biddle 1999, Fold design © Steve and Megumi Biddle 1999
All inquiries should be addressed to: Barron's Educational Series, Inc., 250 Wireless Boulevard, Hauppauge, NY 11788, http://www.barronseduc.com
Library of Congress Catalog Card No. 99-65569 International Standard Book No. 0-7641-1446-8
PRINTED IN HONG KONG   9 8 7 6 5 4 3 2 1

Diving into Underwater Origami

Discover the mysterious world of Neptune's marine kingdom and take a spectacular journey to the chilly ocean depths with paper-craft experts, Steve and Megumi Biddle. *Underwater Origami* shows how, with a little paper-folding know-how, you can make a spectacular collection of sharks, dolphins, whales, and turtles from just a few simple pieces of paper!

Origami Tools and Tips

- Make sure your paper is square.

- Fold on a flat surface.

- Make your folds neat and accurate by creasing them into place with your thumbnail.

- Try making the models in the order in which they appear – often the folds and folding procedures are based on previous models, so you'll find it easier.

- You will need: a glue stick, a pencil, a ruler, felt-tip pens, and scissors. *(Always be very careful when handling scissors and keep all tools in a safe place, out of the reach of small children.)*

- This means turn to the next page to continue the model.

- This means that the model is complete.

Traditional origami paper is colored on one side and white on the other. In the illustrations, the shading represents the colored side. Use *Underwater Origami* as the first step toward creating your own sea creatures, then try experimenting with different types of paper (wrapping paper, for example) or decorate your models with felt-tip pens. And remember, if you have trouble with a particularly tricky fold, don't give up! Just put the model aside and come back to it another day.

Have fun!

Contents

Useful Addresses

Steve and Megumi Biddle, Random House Children's Books, 20 Vauxhall Bridge Road, London SW1V 2SA (Please send an SAE.)
The British Origami Society, 35 Corfe Crescent, Hazelgrove, Stockport, Cheshire SK7 5PR
Origami USA, 15 West 77th Street, New York, NY 10024-5192

Acknowledgments

We would like to thank Kayleigh Sparks for her help and support with *Underwater Origami*.

Sea anemone

This jellylike sea creature looks beautiful, but watch out for its brightly colored tentacles – they can give you a nasty sting!

You will need:
- 1 square piece of paper
- Scissors
- Glue

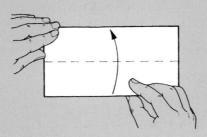

3 Place one rectangle sideways, with the white side on top. Fold it in half from bottom to top.

6 Hold the tube in place with the help of a little glue.

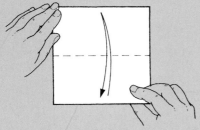

1 Fold and unfold the square in half from bottom to top, with the white side on top.

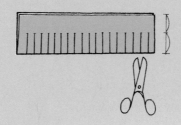

4 Cut slits in the paper, from the bottom (folded) edge, all the way across.

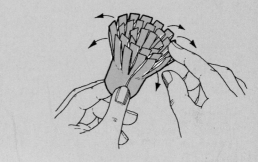

7 To complete the sea anemone, open out the slits slightly. Why not use the remaining rectangle to make another sea anemone?

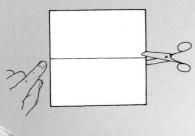

2 Cut along the middle fold-line, making two rectangles.

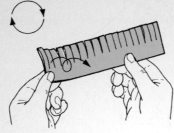

5 Turn the paper around. Roll the paper loosely into a tube.

Seaweed

Try folding paper of different sizes and colors to create a variety of seaweeds — a stunning addition to your underwater world.

You will need:
- 1 square piece of paper
- Scissors

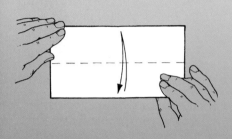

1 Begin by repeating steps 1 and 2 of the SEA ANEMONE on page 3. Place one rectangle sideways, with the white side on top. Fold and unfold it in half from bottom to top.

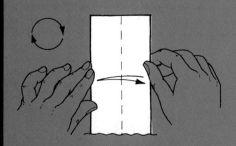

2 Cut along the middle fold-line, making two rectangles.

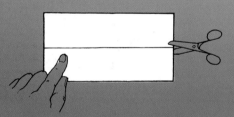

3 Turn one rectangle around. Fold and unfold it in half from side to side, with the white side on top.

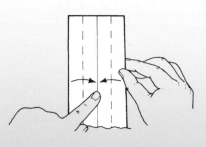

4 Fold the sides in to meet the middle fold-line.

5 Fold the top corners down to meet the middle edges.

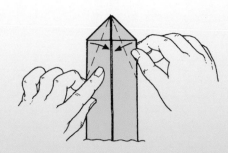

6 From the top point, fold the sloping edges in to meet the middle edges.

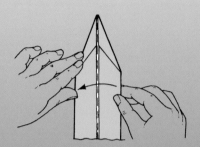

7 Fold in half from right to left, making a strip.

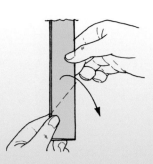

8 Fold the strip down, as shown . . .

Coral

Stonelike coral creatures grow together to form a reef that bursts with color. Use sheets of different colored paper to make a spectacular scene.

You will need:
- A few square pieces of paper
- Scissors
- Glue

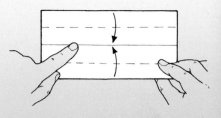

2 Fold the top and bottom edges in to meet the middle fold-line.

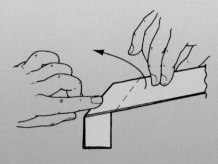

9 . . . and up as shown.

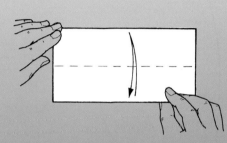

1 Begin by repeating steps 1 and 2 of the SEA ANEMONE on page 3, with one square. Place one rectangle sideways, with the white side on top. Fold and unfold it in half from bottom to top.

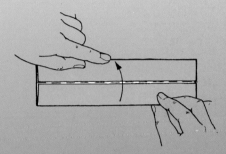

3 Fold in half from bottom to top.

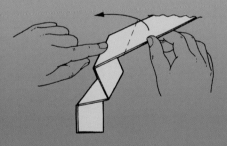

10 Repeat steps 8 and 9 a few more times, . . .

11 . . . to complete the seaweed. Why not use the remaining rectangle to make another piece of seaweed?

Conch shell

The snail-like conch is found on the sandy seabeds of tropical waters. Its large twisted shell is often brightly colored.

You will need:
• 1 square piece of paper

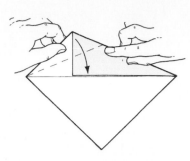

3 From the left-hand point, fold the top sloping side in to meet the middle fold-line.

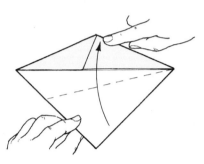

4 From the right-hand point, fold the bottom sloping side up to lie along the top sloping side.

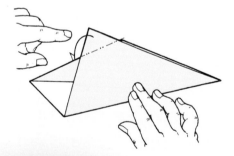

5 Fold the top point behind.

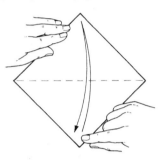

1 Turn the square around to look like a diamond, with the white side on top. Fold and unfold it in half from bottom to top.

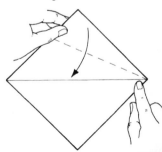

2 From the right-hand point, fold the top sloping side in to meet the middle fold-line.

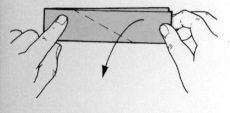

4 Fold in half from left to right.

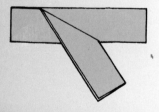

5 Fold the top layer of paper down as shown, . . .

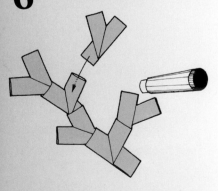

6 to complete one piece of coral.

7 Repeat steps 1 to 6 with the remaining rectangle and squares. Glue the pieces together as shown, to make a display of coral.

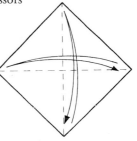

Sea bream

Origami folds are especially attractive when several are displayed together. So why not make a large shoal of glittering sea bream?

You will need:

- 1 square piece of paper
- Scissors

1 Turn the square around to look like a diamond, with the white side on top. Fold and unfold the opposite corners together.

2 Fold the top and bottom corners in to the middle.

3 From the right-hand corner, cut along the fold-line as far as the middle, to make the sea bream's tail fins.

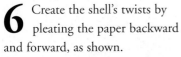

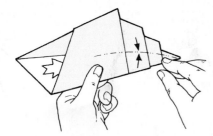

6 Create the shell's twists by pleating the paper backward and forward, as shown.

7 Open the pleats slightly, and shape the shell into place.

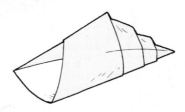

8 Here is the completed conch shell.

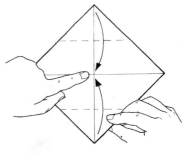

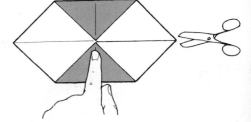

Starfish

The spiny starfish has five fat arms radiating from its body. The fold used to create the star shape is based on a paper-cutting technique called kirigami.

You will need:

- 1 square piece of paper
- Scissors

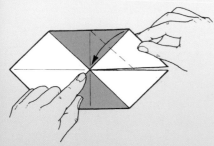

4 Fold the top fin over to meet the middle fold-line.

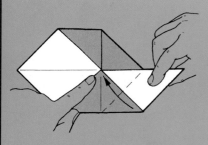

5 Tuck the top fin behind the bottom one.

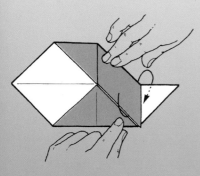

6 Repeat step 4 with the bottom fin.

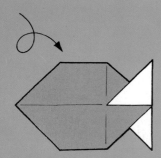

7 Turn the paper over, to complete the sea bream.

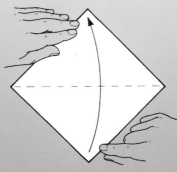

1 Turn the square around to look like a diamond, with the white side on top. Fold it in half from bottom to top, making a triangle.

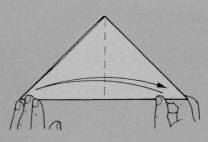

2 Fold and unfold in half from side to side.

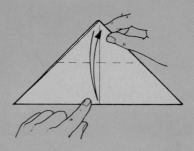

3 Fold and unfold in half from top to bottom.

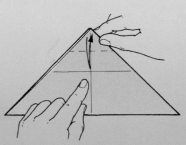

4 Fold and unfold the top points as shown.

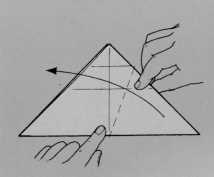

5 From the middle of the bottom edge, fold the bottom right-hand point over toward the left, as shown.

6 Fold the point back, so that it lies . . .

8

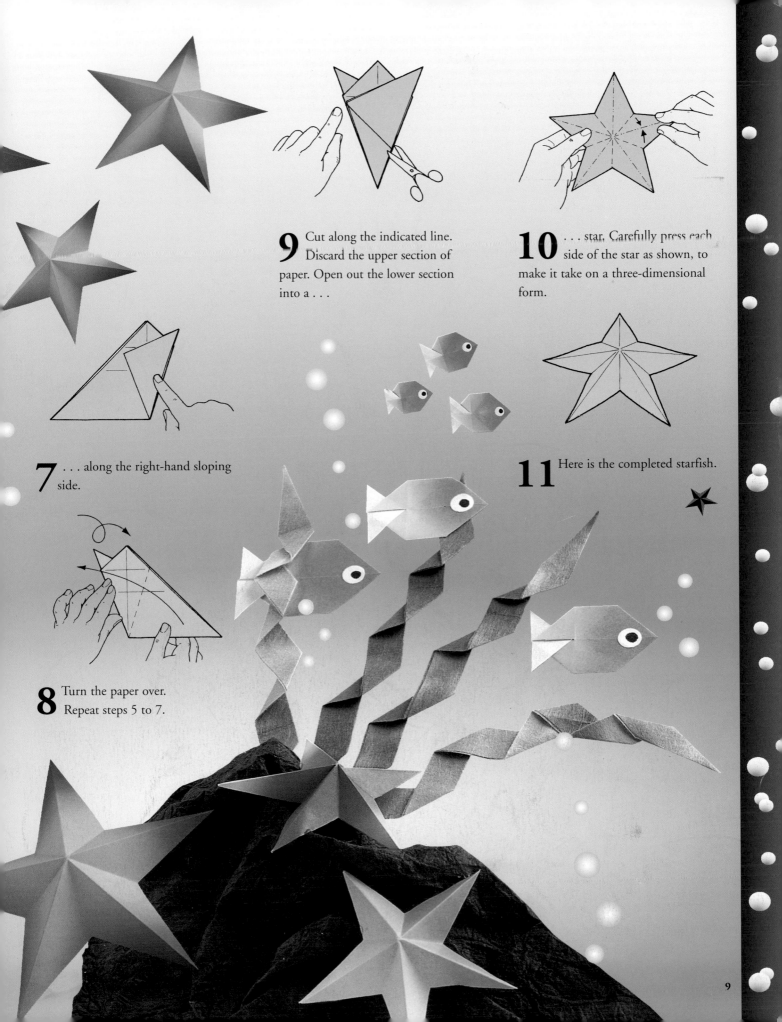

9 Cut along the indicated line. Discard the upper section of paper. Open out the lower section into a . . .

10 . . . star. Carefully press each side of the star as shown, to make it take on a three-dimensional form.

7 . . . along the right-hand sloping side.

8 Turn the paper over. Repeat steps 5 to 7.

11 Here is the completed starfish.

Shell with pearl

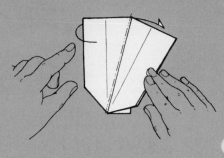

Try looking inside an oyster and you might find a valuable silvery-white pearl!

You will need:
- 1 square piece of paper
- Scissors
- Small piece of foil

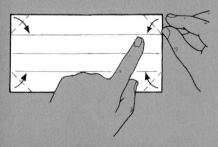

1 Begin by repeating step 1 of the SEAWEED on page 4. Fold and unfold the top and bottom edges as shown.

2 Fold the corners in to meet the fold-lines next to them.

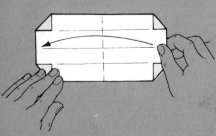

3 Fold in half from right to left.

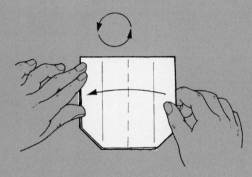

4 Turn the paper around. Fold in half from right to left.

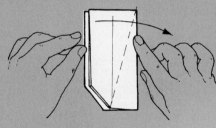

5 Fold the top layer of paper over, as shown.

6 Fold the back layer of paper behind, as shown.

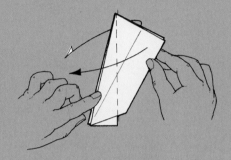

7 Fold the front layer of paper over toward the left, as shown. Repeat with the back layer.

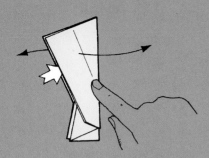

8 Open out the paper.

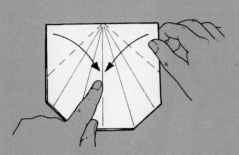

9 Fold the top corners in to meet the middle fold-line, and . . .

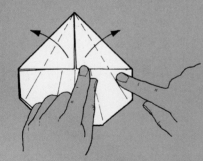

10 . . . then fold back along the line of the existing fold-line underneath.

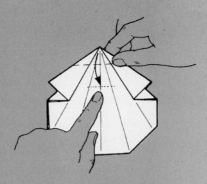

11 Fold the top point down as far as shown.

12 Open the paper slightly along the bottom edge, and shape the shell into place.

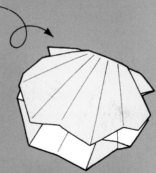

13 Turn the paper over, to complete the shell.

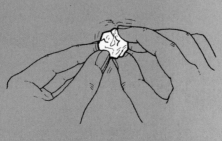

14 Crush the piece of foil into a ball, to make a pearl. Place it inside the shell.

Tropical fish

A shoal of tropical fish is a must for your underwater world – create different species by making slight variations in the folds

You will need:
- 1 square piece of paper
- Felt-tip pen

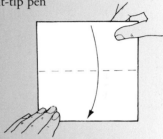

1 Fold the square in half from top to bottom, with the white side on top.

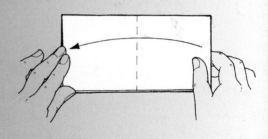

2 Fold in half from right to left.

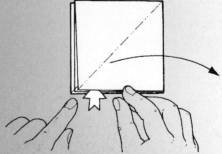

3 Lift the top flap up along the middle fold-line. Start . . .

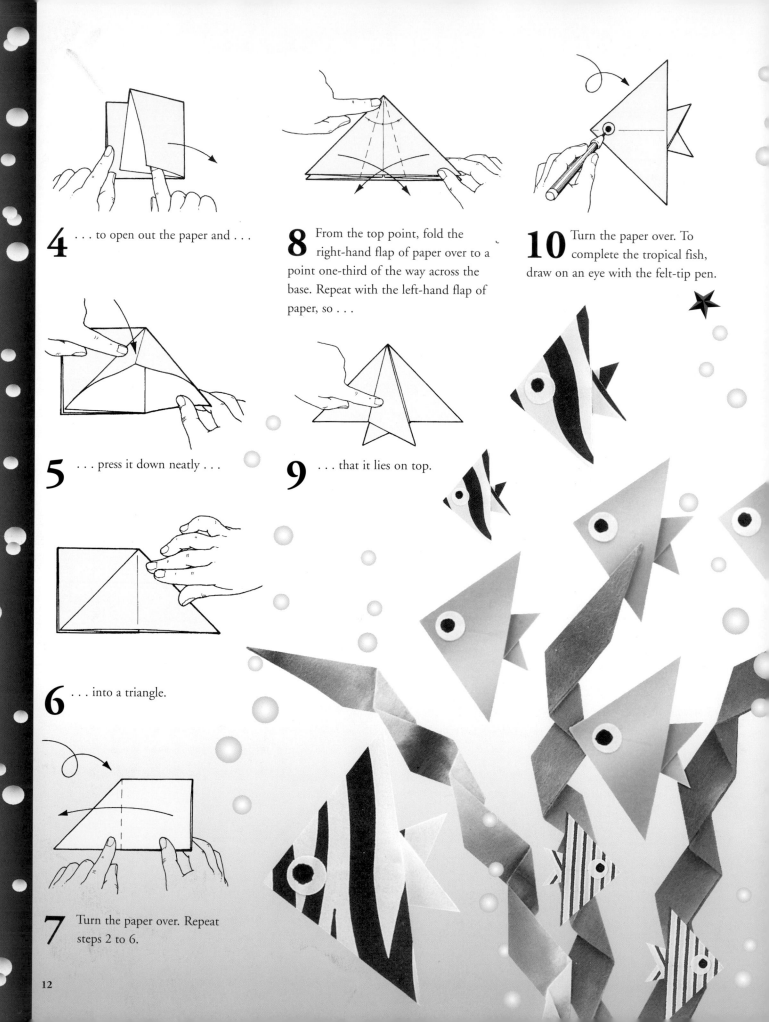

4 . . . to open out the paper and . . .

8 From the top point, fold the right-hand flap of paper over to a point one-third of the way across the base. Repeat with the left-hand flap of paper, so . . .

10 Turn the paper over. To complete the tropical fish, draw on an eye with the felt-tip pen.

5 . . . press it down neatly . . .

9 . . . that it lies on top.

6 . . . into a triangle.

7 Turn the paper over. Repeat steps 2 to 6.

Crab

When the tide goes out on rocky shores it leaves behind small pools of sea water. Look closely in one of these rock pools and you might find this fearsome-looking crab.

You will need:
- 2 square pieces of paper
- Glue

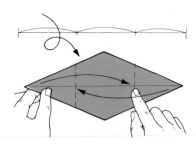

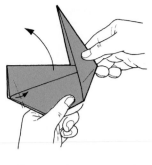

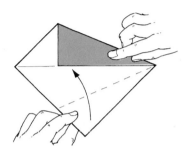

1 Body: Begin by repeating steps 1 and 2 of the CONCH SHELL on page 6, with one square. From the right-hand point, fold the bottom sloping side in to meet the middle fold-line, . . .

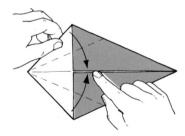

2 . . . making a kite base. From the left-hand point, fold the sloping sides in to meet the middle fold-line, . . .

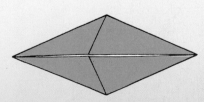

3 . . . making a diamond base.

4 Turn the diamond base over. Fold the left-hand point over to a point one-third of the way across, as shown. Repeat with the right-hand point, so that it lies on top.

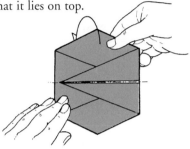

5 Fold the top behind to the bottom.

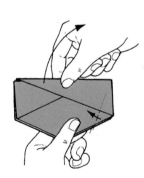

6 Pull the topmost point upward and press it . . .

7 . . . flat into the position shown. Repeat with the remaining point, . . .

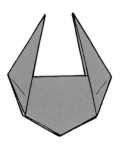

8 . . . to complete the crab's body.

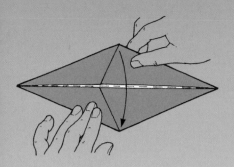

9 **Legs:** Repeat steps 1 to 3 with the remaining square to make a diamond base. Fold it in half from top to bottom.

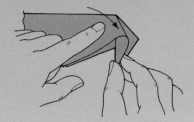

13 . . . the point down inside itself. Press the paper flat.

Mackerel

Bony fish like mackerel propel themselves through the water with their powerful tail. Use striped paper to make a shoal – the pattern creates a very fishy effect.

You will need:
- 1 square piece of paper

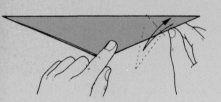

10 Fold and unfold the right-hand point, as shown.

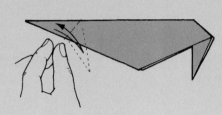

14 Repeat steps 10 to 13 with the left-hand point, to complete the crab's legs.

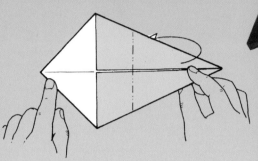

1 Begin by repeating step 1 of the CRAB on page 13. Fold the right-hand point behind to the left-hand point.

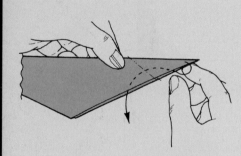

11 Along the existing fold-lines, inside reverse fold the point. This is what you do:

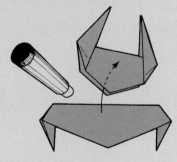

15 **Assembly:** Tuck the legs inside the body. Glue them together.

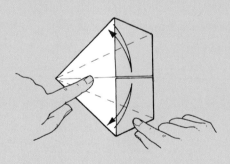

2 From the left-hand point, fold and unfold the sloping sides as shown.

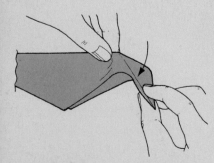

12 Place your thumb into the point's groove and, with your forefinger on top, pull . . .

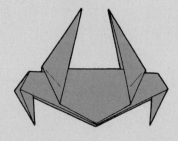

16 Here is the completed crab.

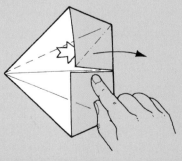

3 Along the existing fold-lines, pull the top flap of paper . . .

4 . . . over to the right, . . .

5 . . . making its sloping side lie along the middle fold-line. Repeat steps 3 to 5 with the bottom flap of paper, . . .

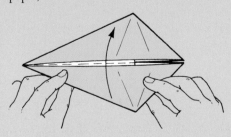

6 . . . to make a fish base. Fold it in half from bottom to top.

7 Treating the left-hand points as if they were one, inside reverse fold them upward.

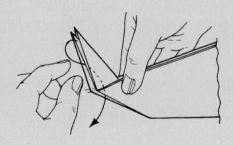

8 Inside reverse fold the inner left-hand point downward, . . .

9 . . . to make the fish's tail.

10 Fold the right-hand point over as shown, to make a front fin. Repeat behind.

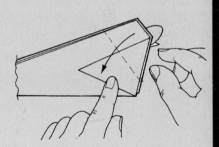

11 Fold the right-hand layer of paper over on a slant. Repeat behind.

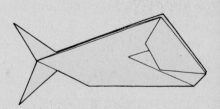

12 Here is the completed mackerel.

Octopus

Eight-armed octopuses like to stay close to the rocky seabed. The largest is the pacific giant, which has an average weight of 50 pounds (23 kg) and an arm span of $8.\frac{1}{2}$ feet (2.5 m).

You will need:
- 3 square pieces of paper
- Scissors
- Glue

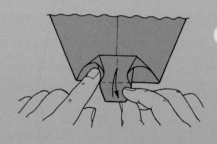

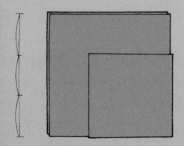

1 **Head**: From one square, cut out a square for the head in the proportion shown.

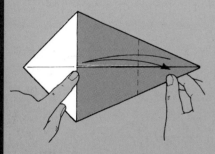

2 Repeat step 1 of the CRAB on page 13. Fold and unfold the right-hand point, as shown.

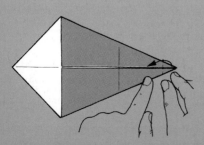

3 Fold the tip of the right-hand point over.

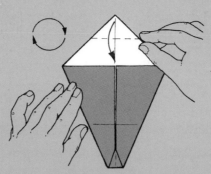

4 Turn the paper around. Fold the top point down to meet the horizontal edges.

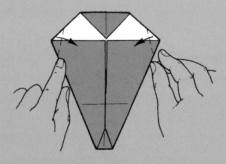

5 Fold the tip of the right-hand point over as shown. Repeat on the left-hand side.

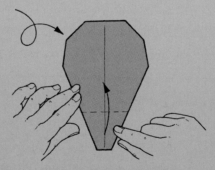

6 Turn the paper over. Fold the bottom edge up along the fold-line made in step 2. Then . . .

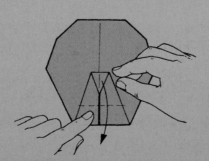

7 . . . fold it back down to make a pleat in the paper.

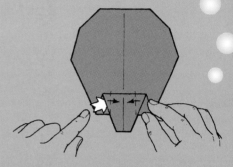

8 Push the sides of the pleat in toward the middle fold-line, . . .

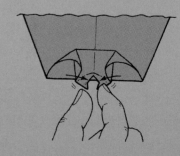

9 . . . to make the octopus's eyes. Fold and unfold the pleat's bottom edge, as shown.

10 Along the fold-line made in step 9, push the octopus's mouth into place. This completes the head.

Humpback whale

Playful giants, humpback whales hurl themselves out of the water as they perform spectacular somersaults and turns.

You will need:
- 1 square piece of paper
- Scissors

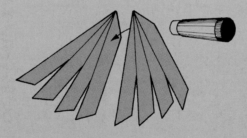

13 Spread out the layers of the upper section, as shown. This completes one set of tentacles.

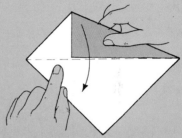

1 Begin by repeating steps 1 and 2 of the CONCH SHELL on page 6. Fold the top section of paper down, along the middle fold-line.

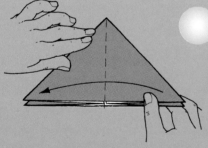

11 **Tentacles:** Repeat steps 1 to 7 of the TROPICAL FISH on page 11, with one square. Fold the base in half from right to left.

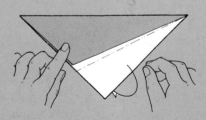

14 Repeat steps 11 to 13 with the remaining square. Overlap the two sets of tentacles and glue them together.

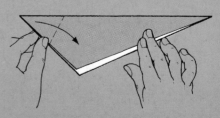

2 From the right-hand point, fold the bottom sloping side behind, toward the top edge.

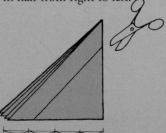

12 Cut along the indicated line. Discard the lower section of paper.

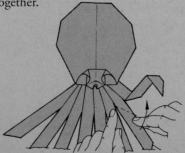

15 **Assembly:** Glue the head onto the tentacles. Fold the tentacles into shape as shown, completing the octopus.

3 Fold the top left-hand point down, as shown.

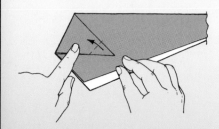

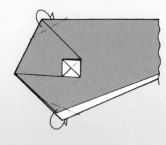

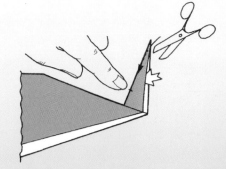

4 Fold the tip of the point over, making a triangle.

8 Fold the top and bottom left-hand points behind as shown, shaping the whale's body.

11 From the point's tip, cut along the middle fold-line as far as shown, to make the whale's tail fins.

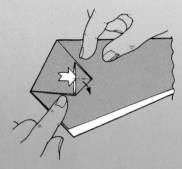

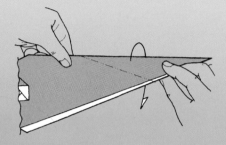

5 Open out the triangle and . . .

9 Fold the right-hand point behind . . .

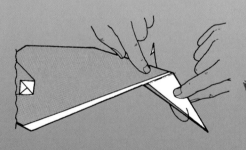

6 . . . press it down neatly into a diamond.

10 . . . and back up as shown.

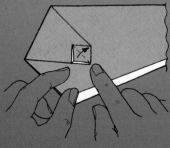

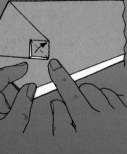

7 Fold the diamond in half as shown, to make the whale's eye.

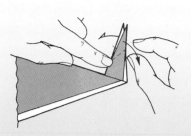

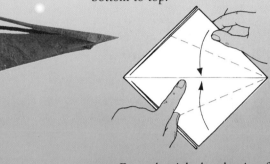

12 Fold the top fin over toward the right and the bottom fin behind toward the left.

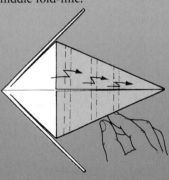

2 Cut along the indicated line to make the shrimp's antennae. Carefully unfold the paper from bottom to top.

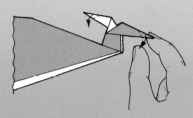

13 Shape the fins by folding their tips over.

3 From the right-hand point, fold the sloping sides in to meet the middle fold-line.

Shrimp

The boneless bodies of shrimp are protected by a hard outer shell. Two pairs of feelers called antennae extend from above their mouth.

You will need:
- 1 square piece of paper
- Scissors

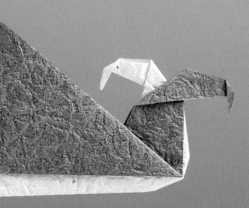

4 Shape the shrimp's body with a series of pleats, as shown.

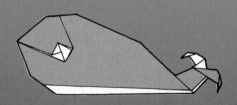

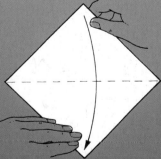

14 Here is the completed whale.

1 Turn the square around to look like a diamond, with the white side on top. Fold it in half from top to bottom.

5 Fold the right-hand point backward and forward, making a small pleat.

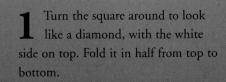

19

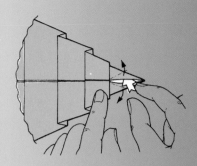

6 Carefully open the right-hand point out to make the shrimp's tail.

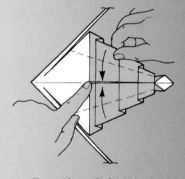

7 From the tail, fold the body's pleated sides in toward the middle fold-line.

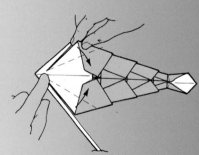

8 From the antennae, fold the sloping sides in toward the middle fold-line.

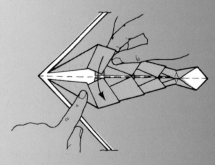

9 Fold in half from top to bottom.

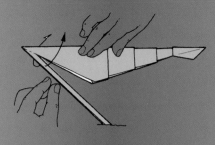

10 Fold one antenna up. Repeat behind.

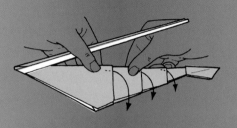

11 Pull the pleats out slightly to curve the body.

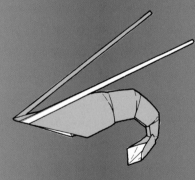

12 Here is the completed shrimp.

★

Dolphin

The dolphin is a small, toothed whale. Groups, or schools, of these sociable animals communicate with whistles.

You will need:
- 1 square piece of paper
- Scissors

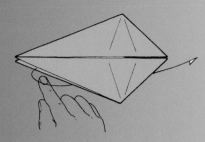

1 Begin by repeating steps 1 to 5 of the MACKEREL on page 14. Fold the bottom left-hand point to the right.

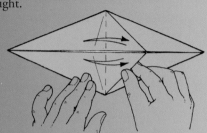

2 Fold and unfold the triangular flaps, as shown.

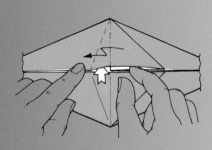

3 Insert a finger between the top triangular flap's layers of paper. Open them out and . . .

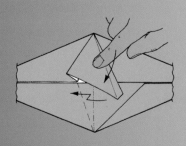

4 . . . press down neatly into a pleat as shown, to make a flipper. Repeat steps 3 and 4 with the bottom triangular flap, so . . .

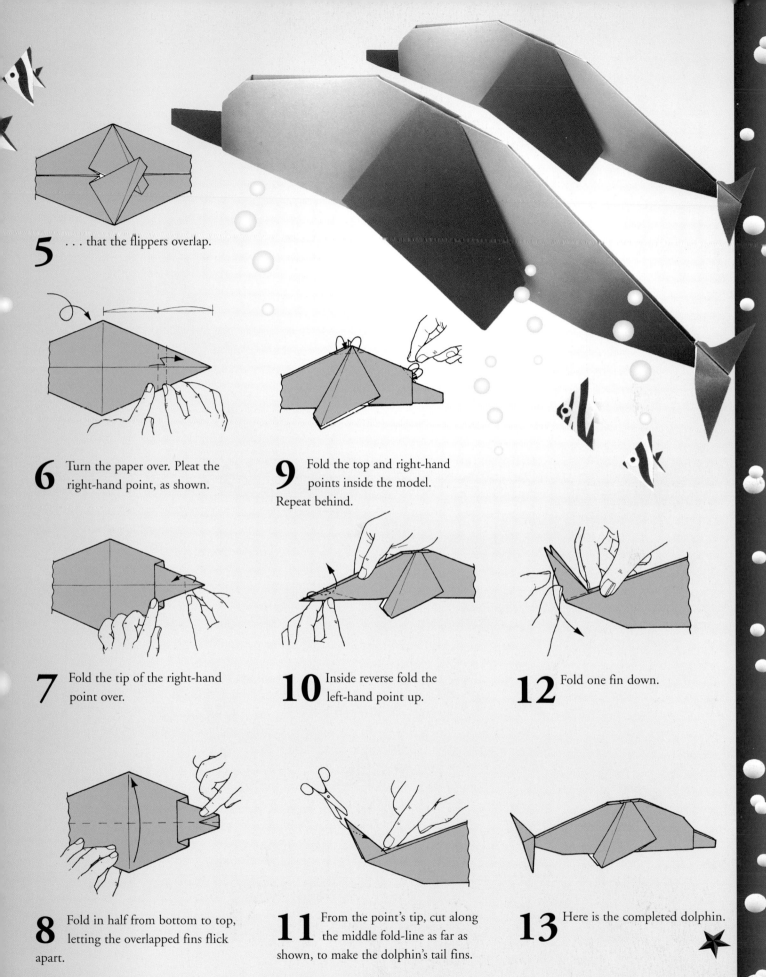

5 . . . that the flippers overlap.

6 Turn the paper over. Pleat the right-hand point, as shown.

7 Fold the tip of the right-hand point over.

8 Fold in half from bottom to top, letting the overlapped fins flick apart.

9 Fold the top and right-hand points inside the model. Repeat behind.

10 Inside reverse fold the left-hand point up.

11 From the point's tip, cut along the middle fold-line as far as shown, to make the dolphin's tail fins.

12 Fold one fin down.

13 Here is the completed dolphin.

Sea horse

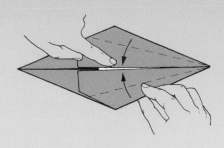

Not a horse at all, but a very small fish, the sea horse swims slowly and stiffly. It stops to rest on seaweed, curling its tail around the stems.

You will need:
- 1 square piece of paper

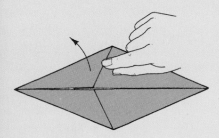

1 Begin by repeating steps 1 to 3 of the CRAB on page 13. Unfold the top left-hand layer of paper.

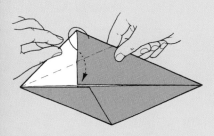

2 Along the existing fold-lines, inside reverse fold the top left-hand layer of paper.

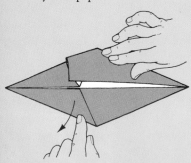

3 Repeat steps 1 and 2 with the bottom left-hand layer of paper.

4 From the right-hand point, fold the sloping sides in to meet the middle fold-line.

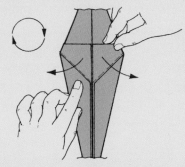

5 Turn the paper around. Pull the middle flaps out to either side, making their inside layers rise up. Flatten them down neatly.

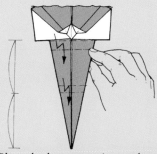

6 Pleat the bottom point as shown, to make the sea horse's tail.

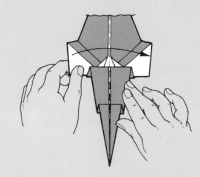

7 Fold in half from left to right.

8 Pull the tail's top pleat out into the position shown by the dotted lines.

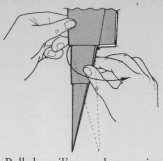

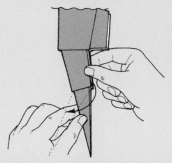

9 Repeat step 8 with the tail's bottom pleat.

10 Fold the tip of the tail over and over, so . . .

11 . . . that it curls around.

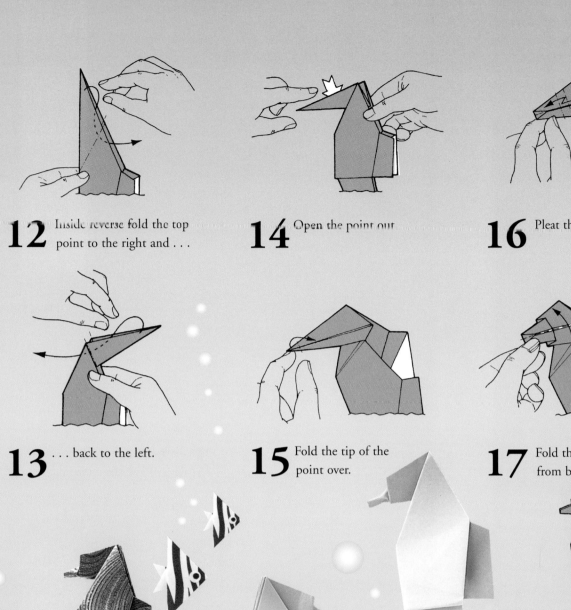

12 Inside reverse fold the top point to the right and . . .

14 Open the point out.

16 Pleat the point as shown.

13 . . . back to the left.

15 Fold the tip of the point over.

17 Fold the point in half from bottom to top.

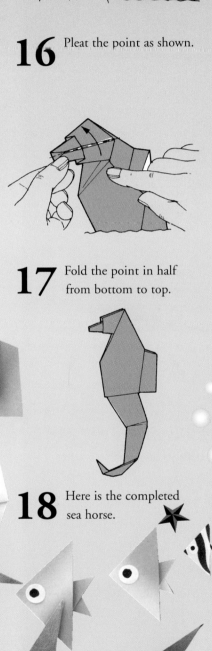

18 Here is the completed sea horse.

Shark

Among the deadliest predators of the underwater world, sharks have excellent hearing and a powerful sense of smell.

You will need:
- 2 square pieces of paper
- Glue

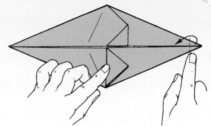

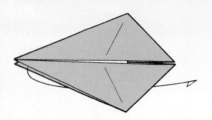

1 **Upper body:** Begin by repeating steps 1 to 5 of the MACKEREL on page 14, with one square. Fold the bottom left-hand point to the right.

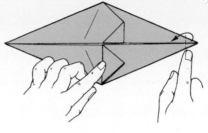

4 Fold the tip of the right-hand point over.

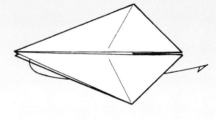

7 **Lower body:** Begin by repeating step 1 with the remaining square.

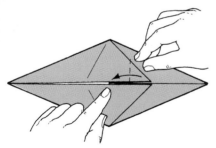

2 Fold the top triangular flap over to meet the middle.

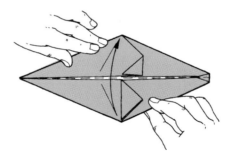

5 Fold in half from bottom to top, . . .

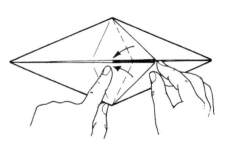

8 Fold the triangular flaps over to meet the middle, so . . .

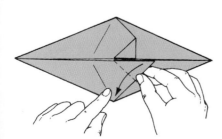

3 Fold the bottom triangular flap down to meet the bottom point.

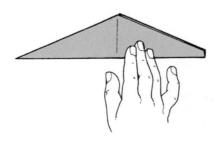

6 . . . to complete the upper body.

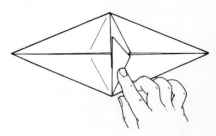

9 . . . that they overlap as shown.

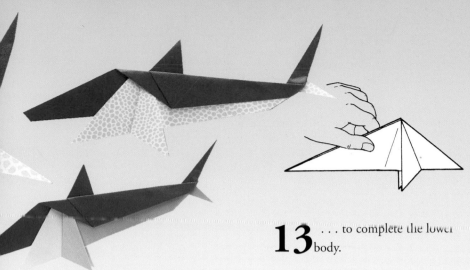

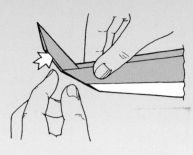

17 Open the left-hand point out slightly.

13 . . . to complete the lower body.

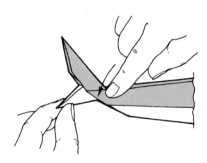

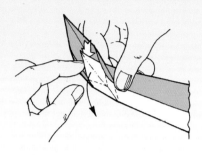

10 Turn the paper over. Fold the right-hand point in to the middle.

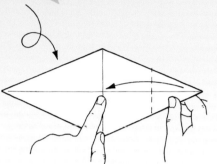

14 **Assembly:** Insert the upper body inside the lower body as shown. Glue them together.

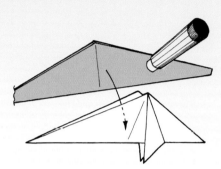

18 Inside reverse fold the inner left-hand point downward, . . .

11 Fold the bottom and top right-hand points over as shown. They will overlap a little.

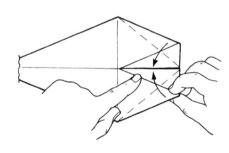

15 Starting short of the bottom left-hand point, fold the sloping side over as shown. Repeat behind.

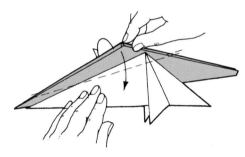

19 . . . to make the shark's tail.

12 Fold in half from bottom to top, letting the overlapped triangular flaps flick apart, . . .

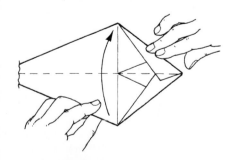

16 Treating the left-hand points as if they were one, inside reverse fold them upward.

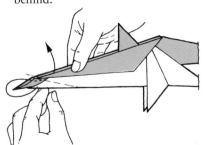

20 Here is the completed shark.

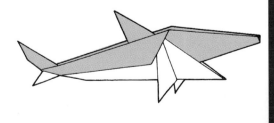

Turtle

Creatures of grace and beauty, sea turtles were swimming in the oceans when dinosaurs walked the earth.

You will need:

• 1 square piece of paper

1 Begin by repeating steps 1 to 7 of the TROPICAL FISH on page 11. Fold the top flap of paper over from right to left.

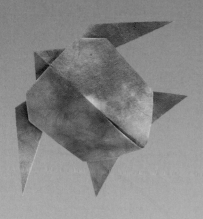

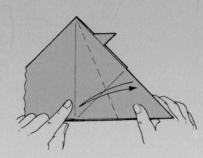

5 Fold and unfold the flap, as shown.

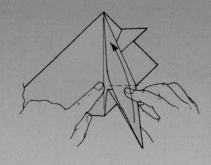

9 . . . upward. Press it flat.

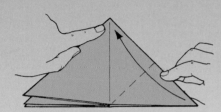

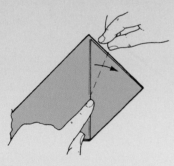

2 Fold the bottom point of the remaining flap up to meet the top point, to make a back flipper.

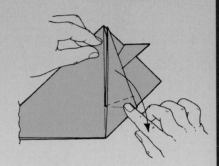

6 From the top point, fold and unfold the sloping side of the flap, as shown.

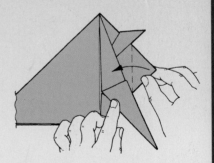

10 Fold the point out as shown, to make a front flipper.

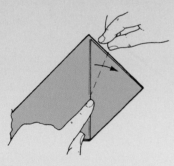

3 Fold the flipper out, as shown.

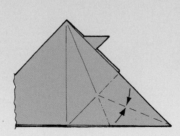

7 Pinch together the sides of the flap and . . .

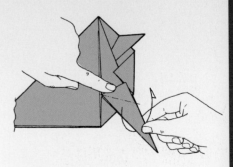

11 Fold the side point in toward the middle.

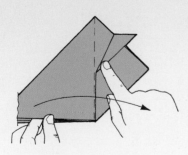

4 Fold the top flap of paper over from left to right.

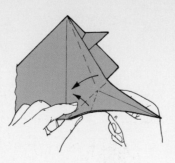

8 . . . fold the triangular point that appears . . .

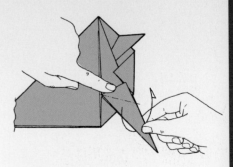

12 Fold the front flipper, as shown.

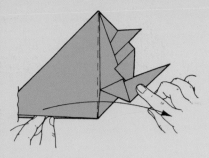

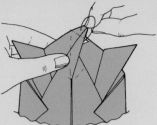

Diver

Once you've made all the creatures for your underwater kingdom, you are ready to make a diver – the ultimate origami challenge. It is made up of similar units, so be careful not to mix up your paper and the steps.

13 Fold the top flap of paper over from left to right.

17 Fold the top point behind, inside the model, holding the pleat made in step 16 in place.

You will need:
- 6 square pieces of paper
- Scissors
- Glue

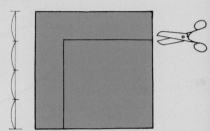

14 Repeat steps 2 to 12.

18 Turn the paper over to complete the turtle.

1 **Head:** From one square, cut out a square for the head in the proportion shown.

15 This should be the result. Pleat the bottom point to make the turtle's head.

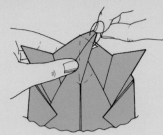

16 Pleat the top point as shown, making the paper become three-dimensional.

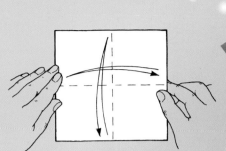

2 Fold and unfold the square in half from bottom to top and from side to side, with the white side on top.

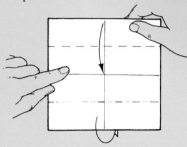

3 Fold the top edge down to meet the middle fold-line. Repeat with the bottom edge, folding it behind.

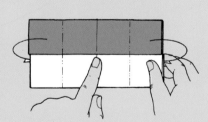

4 Fold the sides behind to meet the middle fold-line.

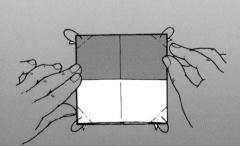

5 Fold the tip of each corner behind to complete the head.

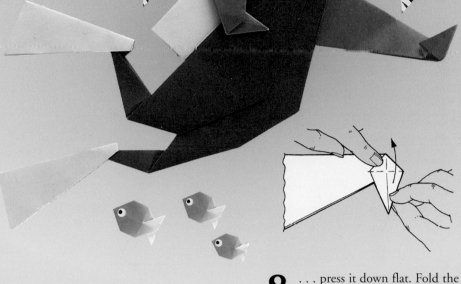

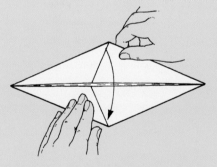

6 **Arms and hands:** Begin by repeating steps 1 to 3 of the CRAB on page 13, with another square. Fold the diamond base in half from top to bottom.

7 Fold a little of the right-hand point over. Open the point out and . . .

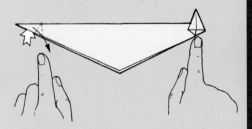

8 . . . press it down flat. Fold the point up as shown, . . .

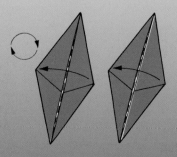

9 . . . to make a hand. Repeat steps 7 and 8 with the left-hand point to complete the arms and hands.

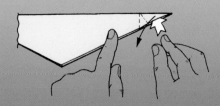

10 **Body:** Begin by repeating steps 1 to 3 of the CRAB on page 13, with another two squares. Turn the diamond bases around as shown. Fold them in half from right to left.

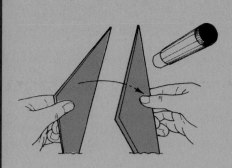

11 Insert one base inside the other as shown. Glue them together to complete the body.

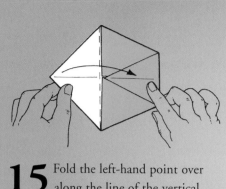

15 Fold the left-hand point over along the line of the vertical edges.

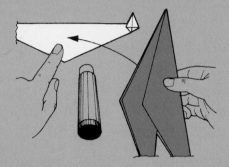

12 **Figure assembly:** Glue the body on top of the hands.

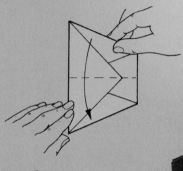

16 Fold in half from top to bottom.

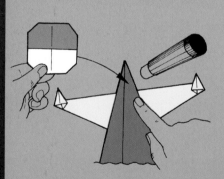

13 Glue the head onto the top point of the body as shown, to complete the figure.

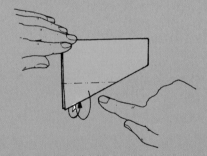

17 Fold the tip of each bottom point behind, inside the model, to complete the air tank.

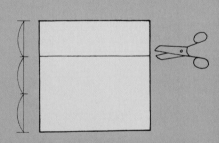

19 **Mask and air tube:** From the remaining square, cut out a rectangle for the mask and air tube in the proportion shown. Do not discard the lower rectangle, which will be required for the flippers.

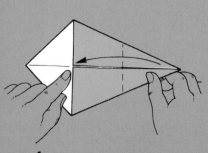

14 **Air tank:** Begin by repeating step 1 of the CRAB on page 13, with another square. Fold the right-hand point over to meet the vertical edges.

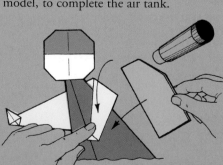

18 Fold the diver's left arm down. Glue the air tank onto the diver's back as shown.

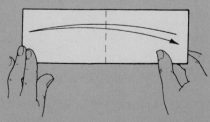

20 Fold and unfold the rectangle in half from side to side, with the colored side on top.

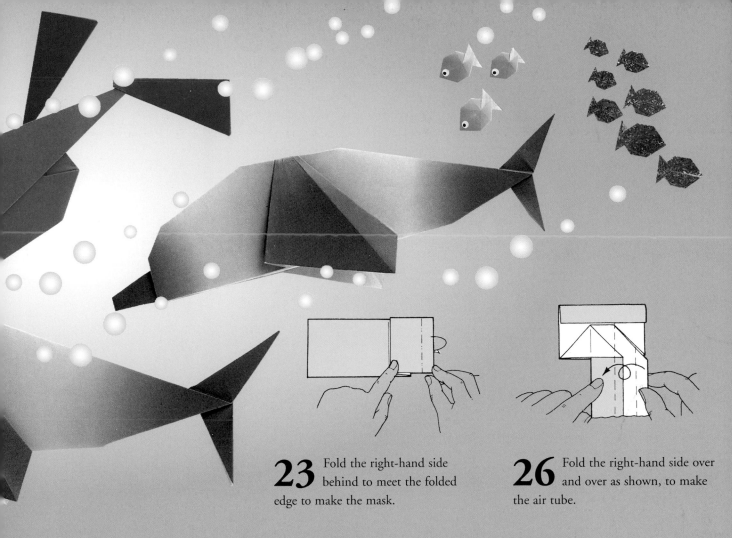

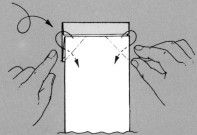

23 Fold the right-hand side behind to meet the folded edge to make the mask.

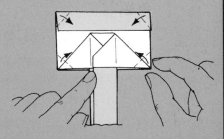

26 Fold the right-hand side over and over as shown, to make the air tube.

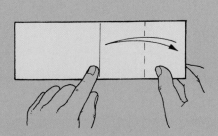

21 Fold and unfold the right-hand side, as shown.

24 Turn the paper over. Inside reverse fold the top corners of the pleat, as shown.

27 Fold the tips of the mask's side points over.

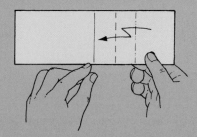

22 Using the fold-line made in step 21 as a guide, pleat the right-hand section of paper.

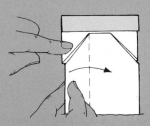

25 Fold the left-hand side over toward the right.

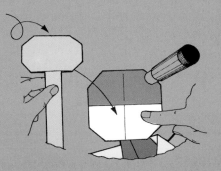

28 Turn the mask and air tube over. Glue the mask onto the diver's face, as shown.

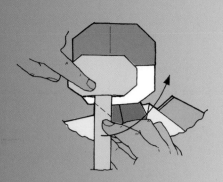

29 Fold the air tube over toward the right.

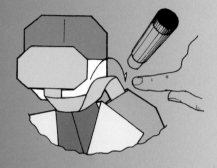

30 Fold the end of the tube backward and insert it into the air tank. Glue them together.

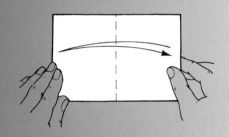

31 **Flippers:** Fold and unfold the remaining rectangle in half from side to side, with the white side on top.

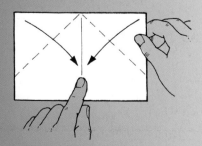

32 Fold the top corners down to meet the middle fold-line.

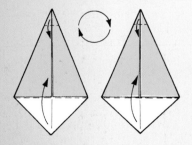

33 Cut the paper as shown, making two squares. Discard the lower section of paper.

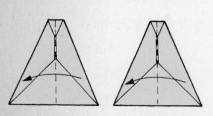

34 Repeat step 1 of the CRAB on page 13, with both squares. Fold the kite bases' top and bottom points, as shown.

35 Fold the bases in half from right to left to complete the flippers.

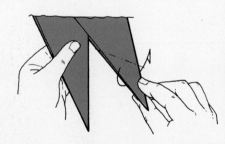

36 Fold the diver's left leg behind.

37 Tuck the legs inside the flippers. Glue them together to complete the diver.